The
Management Guide to
Solving Problems

Kate Keenan

RAVETTE PUBLISHING

Now published by:
Oval Books
5 St John's Buildings
Canterbury Crescent
London SW9 7QH
Tel: 0207 733 8585
E-mail: info@ovalbooks.com

Series Editor – Anne Tauté
Editor – Catriona Scott

Cover design – Jim Wire
Printing & Binding – Cox & Wyman Ltd.
Production – Oval Projects Ltd.

An Oval Project
produced for Ravette Books.

Cover – It helps when solving the puzzle
to make sure you have all the pieces.

Acknowledgments:
Jeremy Bethell
Barry Tuckwood

Contents

This book is dedicated to
those who would like to manage better
but are too busy to begin.

Solving Problems

Much of managing is taken up with overcoming problems which are preventing people from accomplishing their goals.

This can often seem a bit like piloting a small dinghy through narrow straits, without maps, distress flares or a radio. The amount of effort required to recognize the problem initially, track down its causes, find solutions and take action can be disconcerting. It may seem easier to ignore what is going on in the hope that it will go away – it never does.

This book examines some of the ways problems can be tackled, and shows you how to go about making decisions. Once you understand the process, the rest should be plain sailing.

1. The Need to Tackle Problems

Problems usually involve questions or issues which contain uncertainty, doubt or difficulty. That is what makes them problems. But the lack of impetus to do anything at all, let alone produce the right solutions, can often become a problem in itself.

Some people find identifying the problem to be the most difficult part, while others find that working out the solution is the stumbling block. For many, making the decision about how to solve the problem is the impediment, while others resist putting the chosen solution into practice through fear of the unknown.

Not Recognizing Problems

You can be forgiven for not recognizing problems when they occur because they rarely present themselves as a gift-wrapped package, labelled 'Problem'. They have a habit of either creeping up on you when you least expect it, or arriving like a thunderbolt on a hot summer's evening. They come in all shapes and sizes and never have neat boundaries. Nor is it the most important or relevant aspects which first come to your attention. Worse still, they can appear to be one thing while turning out to be something totally different, or something you have met before – but in a new disguise.

Not Facing up to Problems

Even when you recognize that there is a problem, it can sometimes be difficult to face up to the fact. There may be several reasons for this:

- If the problem involves a loss of self-esteem or feelings of shame or guilt, one way of coping is to deny that the problem exists because the reality is too unpleasant to contemplate.

- If finding a scapegoat to blame becomes more important than solving the problem, it is easy to let things get out of perspective with the result that solving the problem takes a back seat.

- If solving the problem means tackling someone about, say, a personal habit or bad behaviour, it may seem easier to duck out of addressing the issues rather than risk a negative or aggressive reaction.

The temptation is not to face up to the situation and to hope that any potential problem will either not materialize or will somehow solve itself. Unfortunately, problems rarely go away; they generally get worse.

Telling others that you have a problem will not solve it, nor will procrastinating, or blaming someone. It does not matter whose fault it is, you need to locate and identify the problem and then resolve to do something about it.

Living with Problems

It is an extremely rare person who has no problems. Yet people often seem happy enough to live with or adapt themselves to their problems instead of resolving them.

This is because solving problems invariably involves some hard thinking. When a problem seems quite small, the amount of time and resources required to solve it usually seems disproportionate to the benefit gained. So the temptation is to live with it or ignore it.

It is only when the problem gets larger that you suddenly find the motivation to solve it. Say, for instance, your office has always been the repository for anything and everything. The place is untidy, but you can usually find things when you absolutely need to. But when Herr Heimat, your best customer from Germany, announces an unexpected visit you are galvanized into action, because the effort required to tidy your office is as nothing compared with the need to give a good impression. Not to do so could lose you credibility and, ultimately, business. It is this that provides you with the motivation to take action.

Rushing into Action

When confronted with a sudden, serious or urgent problem, the need for action, any action, can appear paramount with no time to spend on reflection. This inclination to rush ahead in order to feel as if you are doing something is tempting, especially as being seen to be doing something gives both you and others the impression that things are happening.

But implementing a solution without first defining the real problem is a recipe for failure since you will almost certainly end up solving the wrong problem, or waste energy on one which never existed in the first place.

This means you will not only have lost valuable time, you may have landed yourself with a problem that is ten times worse than before.

Being Afraid of Taking Decisions

Solving problems always involves a degree of uncertainty because, in order to solve them, decisions have to be made, and it is this element that can make them so difficult for some people. Making up your mind which solution to go for can lead to hesitation, delay or not making a decision at all, especially if there are several solutions to choose from.

Fear of making the wrong decision can intimidate people and lead them to do nothing. Yet they often fail to realize that to take no action is in itself a decision on a par with taking specific action.

Once you understand that things will happen anyway, whether you do anything or not, it is easier to take the bull by the horns and make a positive decision, even if it is not entirely satisfactory, rather than let events overwhelm you.

Summary: Resolving to Act

Problems can often seem too much, too big, too confusing to know where to start to solve them. The mistake people often make is in thinking they have a deadline and are required to resolve something in double-quick time. They are afraid that they might get it wrong and tend to do nothing as a result. What is not often realized is that panic itself can prevent people from starting.

All that needs to be done is to relax and clear the mind. Then take a systematic approach and ask the following questions:

- What is the problem?

- What possible solutions are there?

- Which solution would be best?

Resolving to answer these questions makes it possible to take action, and by doing so, there will be no need to wonder ever again, 'Where do I start?'.

Questions to Ask Yourself

Think about how you usually deal with problems and answer the following questions:

♦ Do I sometimes fail to recognize a problem?

♦ Do I find facing up to some problems difficult?

♦ Would I prefer to live with many problems rather than do something about them?

♦ Do I hope that if I ignore a problem long enough it will eventually go away?

♦ Do I tend to rush into remedial action before I have found out what the real problem is?

♦ Am I reluctant to make decisions in case I make the wrong one?

♦ Do I find it difficult to know where to start when trying to solve a problem?

If you have answered 'Yes' to most or all of these questions, you may need to assess your attitude to solving problems.

You Will Be Doing Better If...

★ You are quick to recognize problems.

★ You decide to face up to problems.

★ You are convinced that taking a decision is better than doing nothing.

★ You understand that solving problems involves making an effort.

★ You appreciate that you need to identify the problem before rushing into action.

★ You relax and clear your mind before considering the problem.

★ You determine to tackle problems sooner rather than later.

2.   Defining the Problem

Defining the real problem that you are facing is all-important. What may appear to you to be a niggling small issue may be disguising a huge submerged mine, waiting to be detonated. On the other hand it may be that, like Don Quixote, you think you have to contend with thirty ferocious giants when turn out to be harmless windmills.

So to solve a problem, you need to make sure that what you think is the problem actually *is* the problem. The only way you can do this is to describe its features in detail and examine the causes. You also need to have a fair idea of what you are aiming for in solving the problem.

What is Happening?

You may think it is quite clear what your problem is but in fact to really get to grips with it, you need to define it properly. A problem well stated is a problem half solved. No matter how obvious a problem seems, until you have sized up what is happening, you cannot fully appreciate the extent of it.

This means making a conscious effort to describe how the problem is affecting the current situation as you see it. For example:

The Management Exercise. You are involved in a management exercise and have been deposited in the middle of moorland with a colleague and an ancient clapped-out bicycle. Both of you have to get to a checkpoint, with the bicycle, within 2 hours. You have a map, a compass – and it is drizzling.

The Career Move. You have been unexpectedly offered a job to the Middle East. It comes at a time when your current career prospects seem negligible. Your spouse has been nagging you to make a change.

The Computer System. Your competitors are charging less than you, so you have carried out a business analysis. You have found that your computer system cannot give you a fast enough turnround to charge a lower price.

The Deadline. Another deadline has been missed. The customer is hopping mad. You have failed on a previous occasion to meet a deadline, and instigated a robust scheduling system to make sure it did not happen again, but something must be wrong with it.

Making a list of the facts relating to the problem as you see it helps you to understand it. It allows you to determine what is actually happening rather than what you think is happening.

14

Questions to Ask About Your Problem

Once you have your problem stated, you need to ask yourself the following questions:

1. Do I need to take prompt action to solve the problem, or can I spend time considering it?
2. Do I need to ask other people?
3. Do I need to find out more about the problem?

These could give you the following answers:

The Management Exercise. I do need to take prompt action otherwise I'm going to be stuck on this moor all night and very possibly die of exposure. My colleague and I need to get our heads together.

The Career Move. I can take time to consider what to do as I don't have to give my decision for two months. I certainly need to consult my family because it involves them in a major upheaval, and my spouse has already pointed out that his/her job needs to be taken into account and that our son is due to take important examinations in a year's time. I definitely need to find out more about the location and facilities.

The Computer System. I need to solve the problem shortly because I'll start to lose business. I have to draw up a specification of what is required and then discuss it with others in the company.

The Deadline. I need to make sure the next deadline isn't missed. I must get other people's opinions about why they think the problem arose and I certainly need to find out more about the way people are working.

Once you have done these things, you will then be able to write down in detail or even draw a diagram of what you consider the real problem to be. Very often it is not that people do not have any ideas about how the problem might be solved, it is that they have not spent any time defining the current situation accurately. Like a doctor, once you have a list of the symptoms, you can begin to make a correct diagnosis.

How Did This Happen?

Think about the possible causes for the situation occurring in the first place. Concentrate on the facts available to you, as well as listening to others' opinions. By trying to view the problem objectively you can make simple what seems on the surface to be intensely complex. For example:

The Management Exercise. I'm here because I was foolish enough to believe that it might be fun to prove myself against the elements and had a vague notion that I might make new business contacts.

The Deadline. I didn't keep an eye on the schedule nor did I supervise it properly because I was totally absorbed by another project.

Solving any problem is made a great deal easier if you can identify the root cause, or at least have a good idea of how the problem came about.

What Am I Aiming For?

You need to establish what you are aiming for when solving a problem. You also need to identify what you will forfeit if you fail to solve it. By doing this, you can discover the important and less important aspects of the problem. For instance:

The Management Exercise
Aim – I want to prove myself.
Forfeit – I'll take a blow to my ego.

The Career Move
Aim – I want to stretch myself by taking on new challenges.
Forfeit – I could miss an opportunity for personal development and cause havoc to my family.

The Computer System
Aim – I want to keep abreast of my competitors.
Forfeit – I'm going to fall further and further behind.

The Deadline

Aim – I need to keep a valued customer satisfied.

Forfeit – I may lose the customer, and possibly others besides.

From this analysis you will see that some problems hold considerably more penalties if you fail to solve them, while others have little consequence at all. What appears to be a pressing problem can turn out to be more uncomfortable than serious, whereas what on the surface appears to be a one-off problem may have much longer-term ramifications.

Summary: Specifying the Problem

Understanding exactly what is happening and identifying the possible causes enables you to specify what the real problem is.

By spending time assessing the situation, you will be able to save time when you come to choose what to do to solve it. You will also learn how urgent it is, and what is liable to happen if it is not solved.

Solving any problem depends principally on having a true understanding of what that problem is. Identifying it accurately means that you stand a much better chance of finding an appropriate solution.

Questions to Ask Yourself

Think about the factors involved in defining problems and ask yourself the following questions:

♦ Do I appreciate that examining the problem can sharpen my view of it?

♦ Have I written it down to get a better understanding of it?

♦ Have I thought about why it could be happening?

♦ Have I found out more about the problem.

♦ Do I know what I am aiming for by solving the problem?

♦ Am I clear about what will happen if I don't solve the problem?

You Will Be Doing Better If...

★ You are prepared to spend time examining the problem.

★ You write down what you think is happening.

★ You understand why the problem has occurred.

★ You find out more about the problem.

★ You know what you expect to gain from solving the problem.

★ You appreciate the consequences of not solving the problem.

★ You feel that the problem is satisfactorily defined.

3.   Seeking a Solution

A problem is rarely solved by taking a blind stab at it. Indeed this usually creates more problems than it solves. The instinctive inclination is to choose the first obvious way out – just to rid yourself of the problem. The sensible response is to hold back and not settle immediately for a single solution, no matter how attractive it may appear.

Generally there is more than one possible answer to any problem and the obvious solution is not necessarily the best solution. Rather you should seek a range of options which could conceivably solve the problem, so you can be confident that when you make your choice you will opt for the most appropriate course of action.

Generating Options

Generating a number of options involves three processes: gathering information, producing ideas, and listing the findings.

1. Gathering Information

The first stage in finding solutions is to gather as much relevant information about the problem as you can. You need to try to keep an open mind when collecting facts. For example, with the computer system, if you have a self-imposed constraint on cost, you may miss the ideal equipment for your business which has recently come on to the market because it was just outside your price range, but which you might conceivably have raised enough funds to buy.

You gather information by:

● Asking yourself what you need to know.
● Collecting as much information as possible, by your own efforts and by consulting others.
● Listing the facts you have obtained in any way that makes sense and is easy to understand.

The information that is relevant and pertinent will not necessarily depend upon the complexity of the problem. Often those that seem most tortuous can hinge on something elementary. For instance:

The Management Exercise. You need to know the direction to take, the nature of the terrain, the limits of the bicycle and your collective stamina. (And whether you can rely upon each other.)

The Computer System. You need to know about the different systems on the market, and what they are like from the user's point of view, by shopping around among suppliers and consulting others in your field. Then you need to match the information you have collected to your specification. (It may be technologically brilliant but is it easy to type a letter?)

The Career Move. You need to know about the standards of living, the cost of everyday items, the tax liabilities, the ease and price of returning home, the type of accommodation, the job and educational opportunities. (The climate might be outstanding, but what about the price of toothpaste or tissues?)

The Deadline. You need to know who is not doing what, and why. Consult others and see for yourself how well people appear to be getting on with each other and how the system is working. (Are people competent and could jealousy be a factor?)

How much time and effort you give to doing this depends on you, but you need to remember that if you were to wait until you had every scrap of information, the world would pass you by while you were busy amassing all the facts. You could be in danger of forgetting why you are collecting them and may easily lose the moment for action. On the other hand, not collecting enough means you will not have sufficient data to make the right decision.

Once you have gathered as much as you can, you will have a better and more accurate feeling for the situation and have an informed base from which to proceed. For instance, with the Deadline, you discover that two people are not getting on at all well together which is delaying the work and disrupting production.

2. Producing Ideas

The next step is to produce ideas which will act as a catalyst to getting the problem solved. There are very few problems which have only one solution. Most have a number of answers so all you need to do is uncover them. You do this by:

- **Approaching the problem objectively**. Being prepared to think laterally and divergently will help to prevent you from being influenced by your own personal preferences. You will also find yourself more willing to consider unconventional options.

- **Brainstorming**. Getting a number of other views on the problem from an interested group can often make you see it in a fresh light. This can be an exhilarating process and therefore needs careful discipline, namely that:

  - A strict limit needs to be imposed on the time allowed for creative thinking. (Not too long, to prevent people running out of ideas.)

  - All the ideas put forward should be accepted initially without criticism and without discussion and recorded for later evaluation. (Even a loony idea goes down for subsequent consideration because it could spark off other ideas.)

- Everyone should be encouraged to propose and develop ideas. (Disbelief is suspended while ideas are suggested so no notion is shelved too soon.)

Culling suggestions from other people almost certainly provides you with a wider range of new ideas and possible options that you could never have thought up on your own.

3. Listing the Findings

The final stage, once you have a number of ideas which could provide possible solutions, is to write them all down. Make sure you do this without making any judgement about the feasibility of implementing any of them. Just get them down. For instance:

The Management Exercise
Some of the options for getting to the checkpoint might be:
- Option 1: One of you rides the bicycle, the other sits on the crossbar.
- Option 2: Both of you walk and push the bicycle.
- Option 3: One of you walks; the other rides ahead.
- Option 4: You toss for which one stays behind.

The Deadline

Some of the options for meeting the deadline could be:
- Option 1: Set new standards.
- Option 2: Design improved ways of working.
- Option 3: Discuss the problem with the principal protagonists and get them to solve the problem themselves.
- Option 4: Replace the troublemakers.

By listing the various options which could solve the problem, you can begin to see the scope of the solutions which could be available to you. What is more, once they are listed you may even be able to generate further solutions. For instance:

The Management Exercise:
- Option 5: You both ride and walk. One of you sets off on the bike, gets off after half an hour, leaves the bike and starts walking. The one who has been walking meantime reaches the bike, gets on and in due course passes the one on foot, goes on for another 15 minutes, leaves the bike and starts walking. And so on, until the checkpoint is reached.

The Deadline:
- Option 5: Keep one person in position, but move the other to another department.

Evaluating the Options

Finding the best way to resolve your problem means evaluating all your options. It is a very rare problem that has only one viable solution and, if there seems to be only one, you would be wise to suspect that you have not fully explored all the options.

There are three things to look at:

1. The Constraints

To begin to weed out your options, you can impose on them some or all of the main constraints which tend to govern the evaluation of solutions, namely the:

Cost (How much can I realistically afford?)

Availability (When can I have 'x, y, z'?) and

Time (How long have I got?)

For example:

The Computer System

If Option 4 on your list is a system which offers far more than you have on your specification but costs 50% more that you want to pay, is not available until next year, and requires considerable time for training, you will probably reject it at this stage.

But if Options 1-3 fit your specification, are by happy chance available immediately, and will save you varying amounts of time, they will certainly be left on your list for further consideration.

2. **The Pros and Cons**

After applying the constraints, you will have fewer options. Now you bring to bear the test of pros and cons.

For example, for the Computer System:

- Option 1: The cheap and cheerful system.
  - For: It just about meets the specification.
  - Against: The storage capacity is limited.

- Option 2: The bog standard system.
  - For: It adequately meets the specification.
  - Against: Some training will be required.

- Option 3: The de luxe system.
  - For: It more than meets the specification.
  - Against: The price is 15% more than you can afford.

Serious evaluation weeds out those suggestions which are totally impracticable.

3. **The Odds**

Next you need to filter out the less suitable options by estimating the odds of success for each of those which remain, in terms of how probable, possible or unlikely it is that the problem will be solved by them. This gives you an even better idea of which options are likely to solve the problem.

- Option 1: It is **unlikely** that this system will be able to cope should the business expand.

- Option 2: This system is **possible** as it will do what you require, but there are additional training costs.

- Option 3: It is **probable** that this option will meet your needs, even if it is more than your budget.

Eliminating those options which are obviously not going to provide a satisfactory solution means that Option 1 will be rejected, and perhaps Option 2. Option 3, despite its expense, would seem to provide the best chance of solving the problem.

All this may appear to be a somewhat circuitous and time-consuming process, but it does allow you to get a feel for which solutions stand a chance of working and which are non-starters. If you try to do this any earlier, you will usually find that you just make your choice at random, or favour one particular option and fail to take other key points into account.

Taking a Final Look

Before you finish evaluating options, take a step back and look at the problem one more time. You need to check that you have got things in perspective and have not been seduced by the excitement of generating ideas to provide options for possible solutions to the problem. (For instance, having become so enmeshed in evaluating the range of products on the market, you may now think that £15,000 for the computer system is a mere bagatelle, although you originally intended to spend half that.)

It is therefore well worth asking yourself three more questions:

1. Do I need to find a permanent solution or will a stop-gap solution suffice?

2. Do I need to solve the problem immediately, or can I live with it and wait for the situation to develop?

3. Do I need to solve the problem at all?

So, for instance, when applying these questions to **The Computer System**, you could find that you do not need to change the system immediately as there is an inexpensive upgrade available which will provide a temporary stop-gap. And in six months' time when the ideal system is available, you will be better able to afford it, and it may even have been reduced in price.

Or, when applying them to **The Career Move**, you may find that you make a decision to refuse the offer because, having gathered extremely detailed information, you realized that there are enormous advantages to staying in your present position and combating stagnation by widening your horizons in taking up bell-ringing, standing for the local council and joining the horticultural society. It is therefore not a problem that you need to solve.

Summary: Coming up with Options

Even when you think the answer is quite obvious from the start, it is worth taking the time to investigate every conceivable form of option because the obvious choice may not turn out to be the best one in the circumstances.

If you are willing to generate as many interesting and viable options as you can, you give yourself the greatest possible scope for solving the problem. You also have a higher than average probability of choosing the most appropriate solution.

When you have completed the exercise, you may come to the conclusion that the problem is one you can live with or that there is no need to make a decision until the situation develops. You might even find there is no problem to solve, but this is something you would never have known if you had not taken the trouble to seek solutions.

Questions to Ask Yourself

Consider how you go about seeking solutions and answer the following questions:

♦ Have I gathered as much information as I can?

♦ Do I accept I may never be able to get every bit of information I would really like?

♦ Have I approached the problem with an open mind and generated lots of ideas?

♦ Have I now got a selection of viable options for serious consideration?

♦ Have I weeded out the options by imposing the necessary constraints to them?

♦ Have I worked out the pros and cons of all the solutions and estimated the probability of success for each one?

♦ Do I feel that one or another of those left can solve the problem?

You Will Be Doing Better If...

★ You collect sufficient information about the problem.

★ You analyse the information.

★ You generate as many options as possible for solving the problem.

★ You measure your options against cost, availability and time.

★ You work out the pros and cons.

★ You look at their probable, possible and likely chances of success.

★ You know that there is a solution to the problem.

4.   Making a Decision

Problems cannot be solved without decisions being made. The prospect of making a decision may make you feel that the best method is to wrap a towel around your head and sit in a darkened room with a stiff drink. Or even to hang up a piece of paper listing the options, shut your eyes and select one with a drawing pin. Sadly these are unlikely to produce the best outcome.

Try not be intimidated by the magnitude of the decision or allow previous ineptitude to deter you. You need to look carefully at your options, deliberate, consult with others, and then bring logic and intuition to the fore.

Deciding What to Do

Common sense pays a central part in deciding what to do. By and large, decisions based on logic look as if reasoning has been applied to them. This usually makes them more acceptable to others and easier for you to explain how you arrived at the decision. But if a solution does not lend itself to logic, it can be just as sound to make use of your intuition. Both methods have a great deal to recommend them, yet both have 'downsides' which need to be appreciated.

Logical Decision-making

Making decisions in a logical way is appropriate when you have most of the information you require to make that decision. Taking a logical approach can be very reassuring as you can take comfort from the fact that at least you have been rational.

To make logical decisions you need to:

- Weigh up the options and perhaps award points on a numerical scale to clarify your thoughts.

- Select the better ones from among those you have enumerated and evaluated and reject the remainder.

- Decide which of the remaining options is most likely to provide you with the result you want.

However straightforward this appears to be, the downside is that you can convince yourself you are taking a logical decision when in fact it is a biased one. Unconsciously you could have an undeclared favourite choice amongst possible options. This usually emerges very early when various options are being generated and can influence your evaluation of all the other choices.

For example, when deciding which computer system to go for, a previous recommendation may produce a subliminal belief that a certain brand is the best. Thus, when comparisons are made with other products, your preferred system always comes high on the list.

This means that the rest of the process is really an exercise in prejudice and that your decision simply seeks to confirm your underlying preference.

Biased decisions have the appearance of logic, but in reality are more influenced by personal inclination than rational disinterest. You can test this by tossing a coin to make your decision, and wait to see which side falls uppermost. You may not have realized how deeply partial you were until your disappointment or relief indicates that you had unconsciously already made the decision, but had not acknowledged it.

Intuitive Decision-making

Making a decision using your intuition is often the only way when you do not have enough information. Intuitive decision-making draws on your basic instincts – a feeling you have that something is right, a 'gut reaction' or 'hunch'. Hunches can have just as much validity as a decision based strictly on logic.

There are, in fact, specific occasions when taking an intuitive decision is likely to be more appropriate than a logical one:

- When a high level of uncertainty exists and there is little precedent to draw on.
- When the 'facts' are limited and do not indicate a clear way to go.

- When there are a number of plausible options from which to choose, with an equally good case for each one.

However appropriate it is to make an intuitive decision, the downside is that people are often reluctant to acknowledge that intuition has played any part at all in their decision – because it cannot be shown to be backed by rational assessment. Logical analysis is considered to be much more respectable and reputable. The reason others are more comfortable with a logical decision is because they feel it eliminates the risk factor.

It may be wiser to dress up your 'gut reaction' decision in 'logical' clothes to ensure that others will more willingly accept the decision as being one that is carefully considered. So if, for example, you feel deep down that the career move could be a big mistake, instead of saying "It just doesn't feel right", you might say, "I think that, what with lack of educational facilities, the excessive heat, and the cost of toilet paper, it's probably best for us to turn the offer down". This way, people are less likely to question your decision.

Deliberating and Consulting

Taking time to deliberate your decision can help if you are really not sure that you have made the right one. You can do this in three ways:

- **Sleeping on it**. If you still feel the same way in the morning, it usually means it is the right decision.

- **Consulting**. If the decision is likely to affect other people directly, such as the career move, consulting them enables you to gauge the relative merits of your deliberations, and even to obtain new solutions.

- **Testing**. If you are deciding on a knotty issue, testing different solutions can be an excellent way to find out which one produces optimum results. For instance, when trying to ensure that deadlines are met, you could instigate a range of changes in procedure to see which one produces the best results. It may be that it is a combination of factors which ultimately solves the problem and it is only by deciding to try out various methods that you will find this out.

But beware that if you consider too long, or spend too much time experimenting, the solution may well worsen to the point where it ceases to be a problem and becomes a crisis. The enemy of conventional wisdom is not ideas, but the march of events. Waiting for the situation to develop can help to crystallize your thoughts, but waiting too long can fossilize them.

Never forget that there is one infallible aid to making any difficult decision, and that is: When in doubt, say No.

Weighing up the Risks

There is always a degree of uncertainty when making up your mind. No matter how much research and preparation you do, you can never be absolutely sure that the decision will solve the problem. Since it is unlikely that you have been able to assemble all the information relating to your problem, even for the simplest one, you need to accept that your decision will have to be based on less than complete knowledge.

So there could always be a rogue element which prevents even the best decisions from being the complete solution to the problem. To weigh up the risk, ask yourself the following question: **What could happen as a result of taking this decision?**

If you are not sure, you need to work out the chances of your decision being successfully implemented and list what could possibly go wrong. For example:

The Computer System. If you decide on a computer system which is not standard, it may cause compatibility problems, upset everyone, and make the company less efficient.

The Deadline. If you decide that the two difficult people need to be disciplined, you may just foment the discontent which already exists. It may even cause the next deadline to be missed.

The greater the degree of uncertainty, the more difficult it is to make a decision with confidence. If you can at least warn yourself about what could happen, you will feel more sure about your decision. It may still be risky, but at least the risks will not come at you without warning. You can prepare for them.

Reviewing Your Decision

Before you take action, it is worth reviewing your decision. You can gain a great deal of confidence about whether you have made the right decision by reviewing what you have decided. You do this by asking yourself two questions:

1. **Will this decision solve the immediate problem?** If the answer is 'Yes', then you have made the right decision. For example:

   The Management Exercise. Yes, because once we have succeeded in getting ourselves and the bicycle to the checkpoint on time, the immediate problem is solved.

   The Deadline. Yes, because now I have put in fail-safe procedures, and I've separated the two people who were causing trouble, the next deadline is certain to be met.

2. **Will this decision prevent the problem from happening again?** If the answer is 'Yes' then fine. For example:

   The Management Exercise. Yes, because I'll never go on another exercise again as long as I live.

But if the answer is 'No', then you will need to make a further decision by considering another set of options. For example:

The Deadline. Even though I've ensured that the next deadline is no longer threatened, and the offenders are separated, the general unrest remains because the differences between the two people have not been resolved and others are taking sides. So the problem may crop up again. I now need to decide what I'm going to do to restore goodwill and get the two to co-operate with each other.

While you may be confident that your initial decision will solve the problem, you also need to check that another one has not been created. For example:

The Management Exercise. Although we got there on time, we fell out over which one of us would get first go on the bicycle – and this is a bit of a problem because our companies do business together, and we are involved in a vital negotiation next week.

Summary: Making Decisions

When faced with making a decision, you need to do just that. If you do nothing, something will happen of its own accord and it may not be what you want. It will almost certainly be something over which you have no control.

Logic and intuition are equally valid ways of deciding, and whichever you use will depend on the nature of the problem. No matter how much information you have gathered, you may still distrust the overall picture. If you are in doubt as to whether you should make a logical or an intuitive decision, trust your intuition.

The final piece in completing the jigsaw is to consider the risks. This tends to concentrate the mind considerably, which in turn makes the decision less difficult to make.

Reviewing your decision helps you to evaluate whether the whole problem is solved or only part of it. If the problem is solved for the moment but there is a possibility that it might re-occur at some time, you will need to find other solutions and make further decisions to ensure that it does not.

One good thing will definitely come from making up your mind – the fact that making a decision, any decision, brings huge relief.

Questions to Ask Yourself

Think about the decision you have made and answer the following questions:

♦ Have I fooled myself that my decision is logical when in fact it is biased?

♦ Have I appreciated that intuitive decisions are just as valid as logical ones and often more appropriate?

♦ Have I taken time, and deliberated carefully?

♦ Am I sure of my decision or do I need to sleep on it?

♦ Have I consulted with those whom the decision will directly affect?

♦ Have I assessed the risks involved?

♦ Have I made sure my decision prevents the problem from happening again?

You Will Be Doing Better If...

★ You make a logical decision rather than a biased one.

★ You do not hesitate to use your intuition when you cannot bring logic to bear on a decision.

★ You deliberate about the effectiveness of your decisions.

★ You consult with any others who will be affected by your decision.

★ You sleep on something you are not sure about.

★ You accept that a decision cannot be guaranteed to be the right one.

★ You take account of whether the problem needs a temporary or a long-term solution.

★ You check that your decision has solved the problem permanently.

5. **Taking Action**

After the euphoria of making your decision, you will soon realize that the problem is not necessarily solved. You have to take action to ensure this happens, and sometimes it can prove difficult to settle down to do what is required.

If others were instrumental in helping, let them know your chosen solution before translating your decision into action. If they were not involved in helping you generate the options, you need to let them know what has been decided and why, so that they can assist you to implement it successfully.

To convert the solution into action you need to plan what has to happen. Then you have to put the plan into action and make sure that the problem is solved, taking remedial action if required.

Making a Plan

Making a plan of what needs to be done plays a key role if you are to stand any chance of ensuring that the problem is solved. It provides you with a map to guide you through the turbulent waters of putting your decision into action.

Many problems remain unsolved, not because they are too difficult, but because the vital questions,

'What needs to be done?' and 'Who does what?' were never asked, or if they were, no effort was made to obtain a sensible answer. To obtain answers:

- Make a list of the tasks that need to be done.

- Determine any barriers which could get in the way, such as lack of skills or resources, and rectify this as best you can.

- Allocate specific tasks to individuals and co-ordinate the work.

When you draw up a plan, you need to set out what you want to happen, who will do it, and by when. This gives you a good idea of what is necessary to ensure your chosen solution can be successfully implemented.

Communicating Your Decision

Once you have arrived at your decision, rather than rushing off and applying your brilliant solution you need to communicate it in such a way that all those concerned will accept it. To do this you need to:

- Look at the solution from others' point of view and think about how it might affect them. Try to predict any possible objections they might have to your proposed course of action, such as "We had an upgrade before and it took ages to get the bugs out of it".

- Let people know how solving the problem is going to improve things and sell the solution to them. You do this by talking through the problem and letting people know that, if it is not solved, the situation can only worsen; and then spelling out the advantages which they will get from agreeing to the changes. This helps them to accept your solution more readily.

Whether you are dealing with a minor adjustment or a major change will affect how you inform people about your decision. For example, upgrading the programme may only require you to have a word with the operators, whereas getting people to co-operate may require a presentation on the total re-organization of the office.

Making the Solution Work

Getting the solution to work requires commitment and effort. It is always easier to do this when you involve those who have an important part to play. If you think it is all up to you, you could be taking on more than is necessary, especially if you are putting a solution into action which requires others to change their behaviour.

For instance, with **The Deadline**:

- Ask the two people separately for their personal opinions about what they think their problem is and how they consider it might be solved.

- Get the two people involved together and explore with them how their individual opinions and solutions can be combined into a workable whole.

- Gain agreement on how they will go about ensuring that the problem is resolved.

The more you can involve people in implementing the solution (especially when they are the cause of the problem), the more they will accept the changes expected of them, and be willing to make the solution work.

Plotting Your Progress

Once your plans are under way, you ought to plot your progress to make sure that you are on line and that your solution is working out in practice. If you do not keep track of how things are going, you may find yourself with yet another (and this time, unnecessary) problem to solve. This involves:

- Comparing what is happening with what you planned to happen.

- Sorting out any hitches when things are not going according to plan.

- Making adjustments to the plan if is not achieving the required outcome.

By keeping tabs on how your solution is progressing you can see how the results are panning out and how close you are to solving the problem.

Summary: Solving the Problem

For a decision to become a solution, action is needed. You have to plan how you will go about implementing your decision. Everyone involved needs to be fully informed about what is happening, why it is happening and how they will benefit from the problem being solved.

Taking action means that you are well on the way to solving your problem, which should give you plenty of confidence to go out and look for another one to solve.

Questions to Ask Yourself

Think about taking action to solve your problem and answer the following questions:

◆ Have I made a plan of action?

◆ Have I communicated my solution in a way that everyone accepted it?

◆ Have I made sure that those who are involved have a part in making the solution work?

◆ Have I devised a way of charting the course of the solution as it progresses?

◆ Am I committed to making my solution work?

◆ Is the problem on the way to being solved?

You Will Be Doing Better If...

★ You make a plan to determine what needs to be done.

★ You let people know how the solution will benefit them.

★ You get others to implement the solution when they are directly involved.

★ You have a method of mapping your progress so that you know how you are progressing.

★ You are solving the problem.

6. Your Attitude to Solving Problems

To be good at solving problems you need to believe that the results of your efforts will make a difference.

Even if you are not naturally inspired to confront difficulties you will find enormous satisfaction in producing workable solutions. The secret is not to give up when seeking a solution nor to become overawed by the task, but to anticipate achieving a successful outcome.

Wanting to Tackle Problems

Wanting to solve problems plays a large part in ensuring that problems get solved. Being in the right frame of mind is the driving force that generates the energy to tackle them. It enables you to be:

- Positive in the face of adversity.

- Willing to see problems as opportunities rather than obstacles.

- Energized by the prospect of achieving a solution.

If you take the view that finding solutions is a way of overcoming barriers and getting things done, you will discover that the problem appears to be much less formidable and much easier to undertake.

Being Determined

Anyone can solve a problem well. You do not need to possess any special abilities to do it. You just have to be determined to get the problem solved. This involves:

- **Being objective**. Forcing yourself to stand back from the problem and assess it dispassionately (try pretending the problem belongs to someone else), will enable you to see it for what it is.

- **Being single-minded**. Not allowing yourself to be deflected by other, possibly more attractive, things to do, and refusing to accept that the current situation is satisfactory, will concentrate your mind.

- **Being courageous**. Refusing to be defeated, holding to your own convictions and being audacious in the face of difficulties will help you stand your ground.

It is your determination which is paramount in enabling you to solve problems. You have to believe that not just any solution will do – that there is a right or appropriate solution. You know you have to change something and you want things to improve even if general upheaval is a necessary component of the problem-solving process. It is only by being determined to solve problems that you take control of them, rather than let them control you.

Gaining From Experience

Seeing solving problems as a vehicle from which you can learn means that, even if a problem is not solved entirely to your satisfaction, you can gain from the experience and will be able to do better next time. If you need a reminder of how much you have gained, just ask yourself:

- Have I learned anything from this?   Yes/No
- Am I better able to solve a similar problem? Yes/No
- Do I feel more confident to deal with
  problems in general?   Yes/No

There is no problem big or small that does not provide you with useful experience. And each one that you solve makes solving the next one easier.

Summary: Believing You Can Do It

A great many problems seem awesome in prospect, but in reality few problems are too difficult to tackle. They appear complex and intimidating simply because people dread having to face them.

Getting your mind in gear by saying "I can do it" and "I'm going to do it" will help you believe in your own abilities to find a solution. Solving problems is largely a matter of having the right attitude and seeing each one as an opportunity to gain experience.

Questions to Ask Yourself

Think about your attitude to solving problems and answer the following questions:

♦ Am I resolved to take on problems, no matter what?

♦ Do I try to stand back from a problem and consider it dispassionately?

♦ Do I realize that sheer determination will go a long way to solving a problem?

♦ Do I believe in my ability to solve problems?

♦ Do I take the view that problems are there to be solved?

♦ Am I aware that solving problems provides me with valuable experience?

♦ Do I realize that every problem I solve makes it easier to solve the next one?

You Will Be Doing Better If...

★ You always find the energy to tackle problems.

★ You know that being in the right frame of mind helps you to solve problems.

★ You take an objective approach to problems.

★ You concentrate on solving a problem and do not allow yourself to get deflected by other things.

★ You are not overcome by any obstacles which arise.

★ You are determined not to be beaten by the seeming impossibility of solving a problem.

★ You believe in your ability to solve problems.

★ You learn from every problem you solve.

★ You are more confident about tackling all problems.

Check List for Solving Problems

If you do not seem to have solved the problem you started with, think about whether it is because you have failed to take account of one or more of the following aspects:

Defining Problems

If you find yourself unexpectedly in the middle of a crisis, it could be that somewhere along the line you failed to see a problem looming, or saw it but did not want to face it. Perhaps you were daunted by the prospect of having to do some hard thinking, or did not think it necessary to describe what was happening. You cannot begin to tackle a problem constructively unless you have defined it.

Seeking Solutions

If you do not have any viable solutions, it may be that you have not gathered enough information to put yourself properly in the picture. Or maybe you did not keep an open mind when generating possible options and rejected many of them before they could be seriously considered. Possibly you were so keen to get on with solving the problem that you did not take enough time to evaluate all your options.

Making Decisions

If you find yourself still dithering days after you should have made a decision, it may be that you have not listed the pros and cons. It could be that you are trying to use a logical approach, rather than your intuition. Or vice versa. Maybe it is the uncertainty that is preventing you from making up your mind. Making a decision, any decision, is what you need to do.

Taking Action

If your problem still exists, perhaps you were hoping that, having made the decision, it would be solved without your having to do anything. Perhaps you failed to plan what needs to be done. Or it may be that others are less than enthusiastic about implementing the chosen solution because you tried to force it on them without any consultation.

Your Attitude to Solving Problems

If you are reluctant to tackle problems, it could be that you do not believe you can solve them. Possibly you do not have enough determination to see things through. By making up your mind to enjoy the challenge you will not only solve problems, but learn that they are not as difficult as they seem once you know how to deal with them.

The Benefits of Solving Problems

Solving problems is an inevitable part of managing. You cannot manage anything without having problems to solve and decisions to make. Taking a disciplined approach allows you to tackle any difficulty both systematically and creatively. The more you do so, the easier it becomes. Apart from the obvious benefits of solving problems themselves, a number of spin-off benefits can occur:

- You learn to face up to problems.

- You anticipate problems more easily.

- You can think up creative ideas at the drop of a hat.

- You are better at finding solutions.

- You become more confident at making decisions.

- You stop deliberating and start acting.

By making decisions and solving problems, you keep yourself mentally fit and engage in new experiences. A fresh challenge can charge your batteries and stimulate you into taking action.

Action is a great liberator; you feel that you are getting somewhere at last. The will to solve problems is part of that liberation.

Glossary

Here are some definitions in relation to Solving Problems.

Brainstorming – Getting all kinds of spontaneous and outlandish ideas from others.

Consulting – Seeking the advice or opinion of others. Not an alternative to making the decision.

Deciding – Making up your mind; something you have to decide to do.

Defining – Describing the nature of a problem; the whats, whys and wherefores.

Deliberating – Pondering issues and decisions carefully, but not being deliberately ponderous.

Evaluating – Assessing the chances of a possible course of action.

Forfeit – The obvious penalty for not solving a problem, but all too often not the only one.

Intuitive decision-making – Plumping for something that you instinctively know feels right.

Logical decision-making – Using reason or logic to work out a problem.

Option – One of the ways a problem can be solved. The more, the merrier.

Problem – Something difficult to deal with, but rarely as difficult as you think.

Procrastinating – Doing anything to delay having to sort out a problem.

Risk – The element of uncertainty lurking in all decisions.

Solution – A possible answer to a problem, not necessarily the only one that will work.

Solving Problems – Getting things done by overcoming obstacles and barriers.

Taking Action – The process of doing something about the decision you have made, without which you may as well not have bothered.

The Author

Kate Keenan is a Chartered Occupational Psychologist with degrees in affiliated subjects (B.Sc., M.Phil.) and a number of qualifications in others.

She founded Keenan Research, an industrial psychology consultancy, in 1978. The work of the consultancy is fundamentally concerned with helping people to achieve their potential and make a better job of their management.

By devising work programmes for companies she enables them to target and remedy their managerial problems – from personnel selection and individual assessment to team building and attitude surveys. She believes in giving priority to training the managers to institute their own programmes, so that their company resources are developed and expanded.

By the nature of her work, she has had to solve so many problems (both her own and other people's) that she has no problem facing up to them. However, the part she finds problematic is recognising problems for what they really are, rather than for what they appear to be. Once the problem is properly identified, the rest fits together as if it had its own solution.

THE MANAGEMENT GUIDES

Available now:

	Book £2.99	Tape £4.99
Communicating	☐	
Delegating	☐	
Making Time★	☐	☐
Managing★	☐	☐
Managing Yourself★	☐	☐
Motivating★	☐	☐
Negotiating	☐	
Planning★	☐	☐
Running Meetings	☐	
Selecting People★	☐	☐
Solving Problems	☐	
Understanding Behaviour	☐	

These books are available at your local bookshop or newsagent, or can be ordered direct. Prices and availability are subject to change without notice. Just tick the titles you require and send a cheque or postal order for the value of the book to:

B.B.C.S., P.O. Box 941, HULL HU1 3VQ (24 hour Telephone Credit Card Line: 01482 224626), and add for postage & packing:

UK (& BFPO) Orders: £1.00 for the first book & 50p for each extra book up to a maximum of £2.50. Overseas (& Eire) Orders: £2.00 for the first book, £1.00 for the second & 50p for each additional book.

★These books are also available on audio tape by sending a cheque or postal order for the value of the tape to: Sound FX, The Granary, Shillinglee Park, Chiddingfold, Surrey GU8 4TA (Telephone: 01428 654623; Fax: 01428 707262), and add for postage & packing the same amount as specified for each book, as per above.